THE 7 L'S

YOU MUST TAKE

CHALLENGES

Tools, principals, and practices you must have and teach your children

ER VEN NELSON

Author's Note

I designed this book to provide information that I believe to be accurate based on my personal experience. None of the content, opinions, and stories in this book should be interpreted as investment advice, individual needs, or other professional services such as legal or accounting advice. Seek the services of a professional if you need expert assistance in investment, legal, and accounting matters. This book represents my personal opinions and should be enjoyed as such. Please note that some people's names and identifying details in the text have been changed.

Don't passively read this book. Highlight sentences that stand out. Underline key words. Make it *your book.*

At the beginning of each challenge is a section called "Objectives."

There you will find: Objectives. This is what I want you to have learned or achieved by the end of the challenge.

Erven is the founder of the Seven Lessons Foundation, which helps future generations build character and wealth through mentoring and financial empowerment.

Companion To The 7 L's You Must Take

This book describes eleven challenges that will assist you in translating the insights you have gained (about: finding yourself, setting attainable goals, seizing opportunities, minimizing stress, investing in yourself, the power of networking, and basic financial literacy) into practical skills. Based on **The 7 L's You Must Take,** by the author.

An important note before we dive in: the more complex a particular challenge seems to you, the more potential it contains for your growth.

You will discover that doing the challenges requires a significant amount of time and commitment.

(Erven Nelson's, **The 7 L's You Must Take**, is available at: www.iamervennelson.com)

Table of Contents

CHALLENGES

01 - EGO 1

02 - FINANCIAL EMPOWERMENT 6

03 - LET GO OF FEAR 16

04 - SET ATTAINABLE GOALS 19

05 - STRENGTHS & WEAKNESSES 25

06 - FIND YOURSELF 27

07 - MINIMIZE STRESS 30

08 - INVEST IN YOURSELF 33

09 - RECONDITION YOUR MIND 35

10 - EVALUATE YOUR NETWORK 38

11 - PREPARE FOR AN INTERVIEW 43

DISCUSSION QUESTIONS 48

 ERVEN NELSON

CHALLENGE - EGO

Comments:

What do you believe about yourself?

Your ego is your self-identity. It controls your thoughts, actions, and beliefs. Every experience you had from being a child until now has developed your ego. Your ego exists in your conscious and subconscious mind.

This challenge is designed to increase your self-awareness and positively identify your ego.

Directions:

1. You have 25 tokens allotted to describe who you are as a character. The number of tokens is less than the number of choices you have to make. Although you may think you possess all of the qualities below, 25 tokens will help you identify which attributes you believe are more important than others. Bubble in the spaces next to each quality to represent what you think of yourself. You must use all 25 tokens.

1. Bubble in the spaces next to each quality to represent what you think of yourself. You must use all 25 tokens.

ATTRACTIVE	◯	◯	◯
INTELLIGENT	◯	◯	◯
COMMITTED	◯	◯	◯
LOYAL	◯	◯	◯
FUNNY	◯	◯	◯
MOTIVATED	◯	◯	◯
HEALTHY	◯	◯	◯
CHARITABLE	◯	◯	◯
CONFIDENT	◯	◯	◯
POSITIVE	◯	◯	◯

2. Take the same 25 tokens. In this step, bubble in the spaces next to each quality to represent how others see you. You must use all 25 tokens.

ATTRACTIVE	○	○	○
INTELLIGENT	○	○	○
COMMITTED	○	○	○
LOYAL	○	○	○
FUNNY	○	○	○
MOTIVATED	○	○	○
HEALTHY	○	○	○
CHARITABLE	○	○	○
CONFIDENT	○	○	○
POSITIVE	○	○	○

All of the qualities listed above are positive. You may have rated yourself higher in one attribute than the other, which is okay because a person who sees themselves in a positive light will perform better. When you accurately know yourself, you will make decisions based upon an honest perception of who you are. Ask yourself, "Am I making decisions based on how the world sees me or how I view myself?"

Note Any Insights From The Activity:

What did you learn about yourself?

____

____

____

____

____

____

CHALLENGE – FINANCIAL EMPOWERMENT

Comments:

Your parents' good or bad money habits are not an excuse for how you handle your money. Only you can choose to be financially literate.

The purpose of this lesson is to provide you with essential financial language and principles that will teach you the fundamentals of how money works.

Assets Vs. Liabilities

If you want to earn money, you must understand the difference between an asset and a liability. Assets are resources that make you money, while liabilities take away from your income. The goal is to minimize your liabilities and grow your assets. Think of liabilities like debt and assets like potential economic resources.

ERVEN NELSON

Bad Debt Vs. Good Debt

What is debt?

> Webster dictionary defines debt as a state of being under obligation to repay someone or something in return for something received: a state of owing.

If you are making recurring payments to someone, it is considered debt.

Bad debt is borrowing money for something that depreciates or won't produce more income.

Good debt is borrowing money that has the potential to increase your revenue over time.

Use leverage to take advantage of the bank's money. In the examples below, I will show you how to convert bad debt into good debt.

Examples of bad debt:	Examples of good debt:
1. Single Family Home	1. Rental Property (earning income greater than the monthly installments)
2. Automobile Loan	2. Automobile Loan (used as a taxi service earning income greater than the monthly installments)
3. Student Loans	3. Student Loans (to obtain education)
4. Credit Cards	4. Business Loans (to launch and or grow your business)

Examples of bad debt converted into good debt:

1. Residential property loans can be good debt if you plan to rent the property out to earn residual income or acquire a residence with potential equity. Say your mortgage is $1,000 a month, but you rent out the entire property for $1,500 a month. The property is an asset because it's making you an extra $500 a month. You are purchasing an asset that retains some value, providing that the interest plus principal is affordable. It enables you to buy an expensive investment before saving for the whole amount. Another example of converting a residential property into good debt is hosting your property with companies like Airbnb.

2. Automobiles are needed to get you to and from work, but the interest rate is a waste of money. The vehicle depreciates the moment you drive off the car lot. Purchase the least expensive, most reliable vehicle and pay it off quickly. You can convert your car into an asset by renting it out or turning your vehicle into an independent taxi service with Uber or Lyft. Another example of converting your automobile into an investment is building a small car-sharing business with companies like Turo.

3. Student loans are a liability, but education is an asset. The more education you have, the greater your potential to earn money. If you don't finish school or pass your classes, it would be considered a liability because you will have student loan debt without having learned anything. Educators and first responders go through years of study and acquire large sums of debt, but they are passionate about working in their field.

How do you want your life to look?

Some people find happiness in simply going to work every day. Don't feel discouraged if you have student loan debt; plan to pay it off in small installments.

Remember that you are building an investment into a career and a future in education.

4. Credit cards can be a source of good debt if you build a good credit history. You can leverage your good credit history to get approved for the items listed in the "examples of good debt" section above. The longer you have been using your credit, the better. Don't overspend, and most importantly, pay your bills on time. Don't make large purchases with your credit card that you can't afford to pay back in a timely fashion. With good credit history, you can leverage your credit to purchase a home, start a business, or purchase a vehicle with low interest rates. If you desire to purchase a vehicle, I prefer purchasing an inexpensive, reliable car with cash or one that you can pay off quickly.

You are probably asking, "How can I establish credit with a poor credit history?"

One way to build credit is by applying for a secured credit card. Deposit money into a secured credit card account, and your credit limit will equal that amount. Make consistent payments on time to avoid paying any interest. Over time, your credit score will increase tremendously. The goal is to pull from your line of credit to assess opportunities without selling your assets.

For example, I deposited $400.00 into a secured credit card account, so my credit limit equaled that amount. My credit score improved over three months because I made consistent payments. I avoided paying high interest rates by making payments before the deadline and not exhausting more than 30% of the limit. Eventually, I was offered credit cards from other banks because I had established good credit history.

I created the "Ring of Wealth" to help you manage and grow your income by closely monitoring your spending and saving habits. It's time to get out of debt and join the Ring of Wealth.

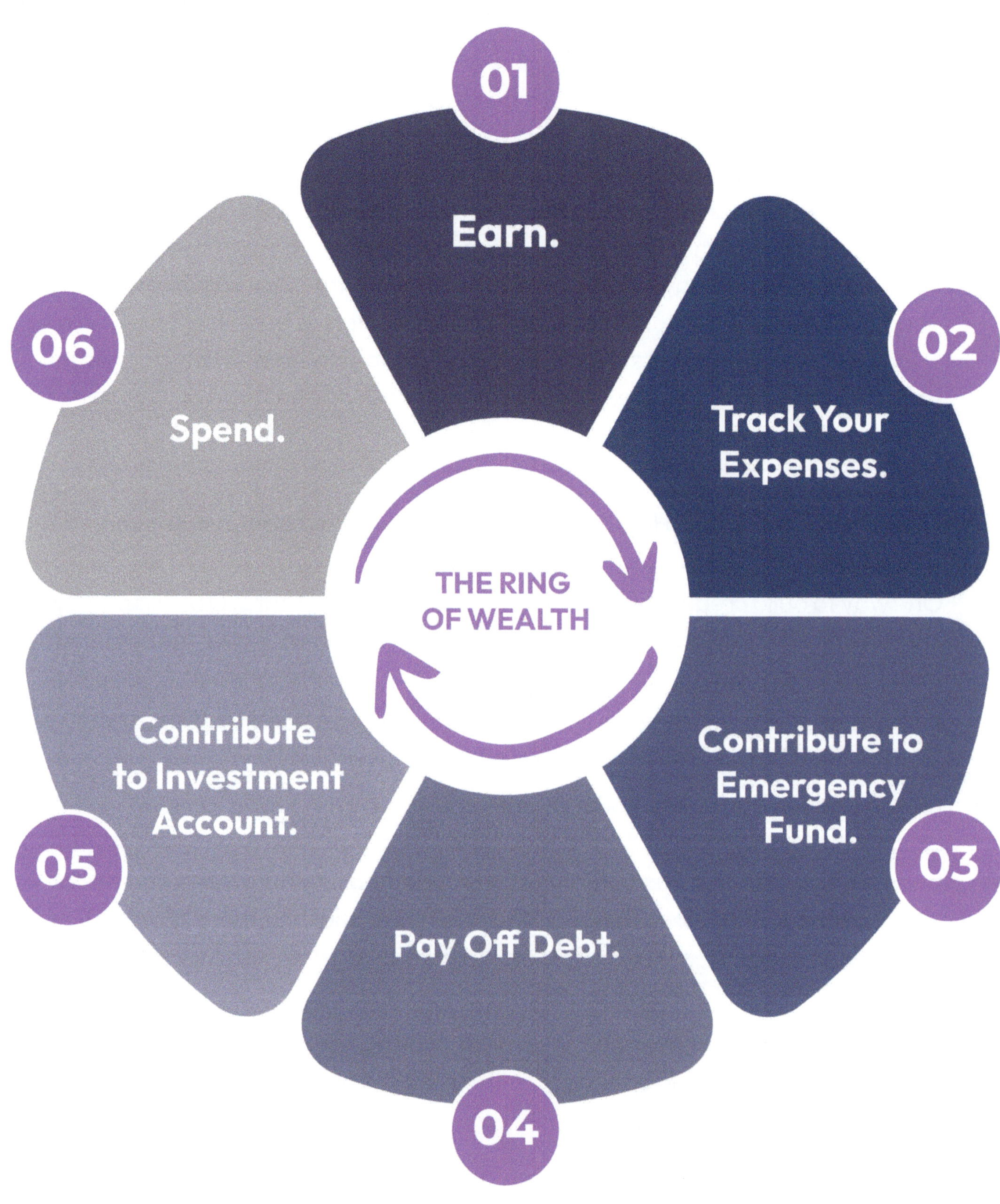
01
Earn.
06
Spend.
02
Track Your
Expenses.
THE RING
OF WEALTH
Contribute
to Investment
Account.
05
Contribute to
Emergency
Fund.
03
Pay Off Debt.
04

Directions:

1. **Earn.** Find work and start earning money.

   What part of the job search process is giving you the most trouble?

   ____

   ____

   ____

   ____

   ____

   Are you limiting your search?

   YES ◯   NO ◯

Do you follow up after sending out your resume?

YES ◯   NO ◯

How do your social media profiles look?

OUTDATED ◯   UPDATED ◯   NOT ON
                             SOCIAL
                             MEDIA ◯

2. **Track your expenses.** List your monthly net income and expected payments on the expense sheet below to help you track your spending habits. Net income is your take-home pay. Gross income is what employees earn before taxes, benefits, and other payroll deductions are withheld from their wages.

My Expense Sheet		
Monthly Net Income		$
Monthly Expenses	Due Date	Total
		$
		$
		$
		$
		$
		$
		$
		$
		$
		$
		$
		$
		$
	Total	$

Subtract your monthly expenses from your monthly net income. The balance is what's left over after all costs are covered.

Monthly Gross Income (MGI)		$
Monthly Expenses (ME)		$
Balance (B)		$

3. **Contribute to an emergency fund.** An emergency fund is monies set aside to cover unexpected financial surprises. Unexpected financial emergencies might be a car accident, medical issue, loss of employment, a tree falling on your house, or your car breaking down. It's not a matter of if, but when a financial emergency occurs.

   Set your emergency fund goal to a minimum of 3 months' expenses.

   Multiply your net income by 10% to get your emergency fund contribution every time you get paid.

TIP

Once your paycheck hits your checking account, it's a good idea to have your bank account set to automatically send 10% from your checking account to your emergency fund.

4. **Pay off debt.** List all of your debt except for your mortgage. When you're in debt with your mortgage, you decide when to pay the money back. When you're in credit card debt, the lender chooses when you have to pay it back. Keep in mind the mortgage interest costs can be tax-deductible, so the government can help out by lowering your tax bill. Pick the debt with the

ERVEN NELSON

highest interest first and eliminate it. Once the high-interest debt is paid off (credit cards, student loans, etc.), you will have extra money to increase the dollar amount on monthly payments for other debt.

Pay your mortgage off early. If you have a 30-year mortgage at 4% interest for $300,000, your monthly payment is $1,432.25. Suppose you put an additional $400 into these payments with the same term, principal, and interest rate. You can pay off your mortgage in approximately 19 years and two months. You would eliminate almost 11 years of debt, saving you roughly $81,099.00 in interest. So if you have extra money lying around, pay more toward your principal.

5. **Contribute to an investment account.** Now that you have your emergency fund set aside and bad debt paid off, save up at least 10% of your earnings each pay period in your investment account for the long run. An investment account is monies that are aside to invest in assets. Think of it as paying yourself first.

Each pay period, multiply your net income by 10%, which will result in your investment account contribution.

Once your paycheck hits your checking account, it's a good idea to have your bank account set to automatically send 10% from your checking account to your investment account electronically.

6. **Spend.** When you make it to this step, you can take the vacation you always dreamed of or take your partner to a "pricey" restaurant—you know, like the ones with tablecloths.

CHALLENGE - LET GO OF FEAR

Comments:

There are many fears in this world, but we all have one roadblock that gets in the way of the goals we strive to accomplish. You will reach your highest potential when you let go of the fear of getting started or not being good enough. I challenge you to make choices fueled by positive intentions, not fear.

I challenge you to make the leap on any goal or idea you desired but never fully committed to accomplishing.

Directions:

1. Think about why you fear taking the first step towards your goal or idea. In the space below, write down these fears in every second line. (This leaves room to write a sentence or two by each fear.)

____

____

____

____

____

2. Assess what you need to conquer your fears below.

____

____

____

____

____

3. Before you worry about actions, organize the steps needed to overcome your fears to a timeframe. (Such as a calendar or numbered order.)

____

____

____

____

____

4. Now that you know what steps you need to conquer your fears, take action. Commit to executing within your timeframe.

____

____

____

____

ERVEN NELSON

CHALLENGE - SET ATTAINABLE GOALS

> Motivation is like drinking a double espresso: it gets you going for a while, but eventually, you'll crash. The key is staying motivated by setting attainable goals that will help you stay focused until you reach your desired results.
>
> **Erven Nelson**

Comments:

Before you can achieve your goals, you must have a plan. That plan is your step-by-step process of small, achievable goals. Goals give you direction, and the plan keeps you focused. I created the VALUE system to help you develop efficient goals and a plan to execute them.

VALUE System: Creating efficient goals and the plan to execute them. If you are willing to try this technique, read the insight and information below. You must implement it in your life every day.

Directions:

1. **Vision:** Create a mental image of what you want to happen. Once you have a clear picture of your goal, write it down in the "Vision" box below. You must align your vision with your plan. It will encourage you to keep going when you encounter a setback on your journey.

   Having a vision will put you 20% closer to accomplishing your goal.

2. **Actions:** In the box below labeled "Actions," draw up and execute a plan to reach your desired goal. Be sure to organize timeframes to get stuff done. Don't worry about making it complicated. Just something that you can easily understand.

Actions

Executing the plan above is the key to your success. One way to execute your goal is by breaking it down into smaller, achievable goals. For example, when I clean the kitchen in my house, I divide the area into three sections and work on one task at a time. I start with the dishes, then wipe down the counters and equipment. Lastly, I sweep and mop the floors. This process ensures progress without procrastination.

Decide on a date to update the progress of your goal. You may have to change the deadline or rewrite the plan entirely due to economic reasons or market changes. Drawing up and executing a plan puts you 40% closer to accomplishing your goal.

3. **Loyalty:** On the lines below, sign your signature to make a firm commitment to the plan you created in the previous step. Your pledge will help you overcome the obstacles on your journey to accomplishing your goal and any other potential resistance to change. By signing on the lines, you are committing to the execution of your plan, no matter what.

____

____

Committing to your plan puts you 60% closer to achieving your goal.

ERVEN NELSON

4. **Unity:** Identify the team of people you need to collaborate with to get closer to accomplishing your goal. Write their names in the columns below.

5. **Evaluate:** In the box below, write your progress towards your goal. (It can be the number of tasks done or what you accomplished up to the date you committed to.) Review your plan and be open to making required changes when they do not happen. This step will provide some accountability and allow you to grow. Be positive during the change process and view change as an opportunity for development.

Evaluate

The evaluation period will give you a better understanding of your mistakes and help you consider possible paths for improvement. During this process, consistently communicate results to your team and celebrate the little wins until you complete your goal.

When the goal is complete, you will reach the 100% mark.

CHALLENGE - STRENGTHS & WEAKNESSES

1. In the boxes below, clearly identify your strengths and weaknesses. Strengths are things you can use to push yourself forward. Weaknesses are areas you need to improve on. You must work on your weaknesses and make them as strong as possible while also developing your strengths. Consider bringing someone else on your team whose strengths align with your weaknesses to help you win.

2. **Reflect.** Reflection enables long-term improvement of all strengths and weaknesses because it gives you a better understanding of yourself and helps you consider a different approach for improvement.

ERVEN NELSON

CHALLENGE - FIND YOURSELF

Comments:

When you identify what makes your life meaningful, it gives you something to strive for each day. It gives you purpose. This challenge will help reveal who you are meant to be, which will lead to remarkable results.

Directions:

1. Write down what you find meaningful in your life.

____

____

____

____

____

2. Write a series of short sentences that best describe why you find these things important in your life. Be specific.

____

____

____

____

____

3. Every time you make a choice, ask yourself, "Is this decision I'm making in line with my vision of myself?"

4. Review this challenge once a week for four weeks. Each week, assess where you are in your life. All the pain, suffering, loss, and failure have contributed to who you are today. Instead of saying, "Life isn't fair," I want you to turn your experiences into motivation and valuable lessons that help you grow.

07

CHALLENGE - MINIMIZE STRESS

Comments:

Stress can lead to health conditions like depression, anxiety, and high blood pressure. I've created the Three P's Method to help you minimize or avoid some of the stress in your life. I have used this method time after time, and it is how I survive overwhelming circumstances. If you are ready to test this technique, read the steps below.

In most cases, you feel stressed because your perspective cannot generate an answer to how you will get through a seemingly challenging circumstance. Your mind cannot determine the difference between perceived negative and actual negative stressors. For example, let's say you are lying in bed thinking about an adverse event so much that you can feel the emotional stress of it. As a result, your body reacts the same way as if you were there.

There are many different types of stress. In this lesson, I will refer to acute stress. Webster's dictionary defines acute stress as intensifying conditions leading to a culmination or breaking point. If you are experiencing chronic stress or you find yourself unable to cope with everyday life, please consult with a professional.

Three P's Method

Directions:

Step 1.

Plot. Take deep breaths in and out until you feel released internally. Dwelling on the problem at hand won't make your life any better. It would be best if you had a solution. Identify what caused you to feel stressed, and create a plan for how you will get out of your situation. This step can be incredibly challenging, but I know you can do it.

Step 2.

Positive Thinking. Challenge yourself to view the perceived stressful circumstance with a positive eye. I want you to think of one experience in your life that made you feel exceptionally grateful. It could be big or small.

Write it down:

____

____

____

____

____

The purpose of this step is for you to subtitle negative thoughts with gratitude. You created the plan in the first P, so here, in the second P, you are strengthening your mentality, which leads to the third P.

Step 3.

Perseverance. Stress is temporary, so don't give up too soon because you won't allow yourself to get through it.

08

CHALLENGE - INVEST IN YOURSELF

Comments:

If you discipline yourself, you will notice a difference. It won't be easy to eliminate old habits that usually consume your time, but focus and determination will bring you closer to accomplishing your goal.

Directions:

1. In the boxes below, list four trades or skills you possess that have value and potential. Now put them in order by priority. Prioritize what matters to you; what you consider your purpose. In the first box, write down the more important one. For example, if you play an instrument, write down "musician." Conversely, write down "auto mechanic" if you repair or maintain vehicles.

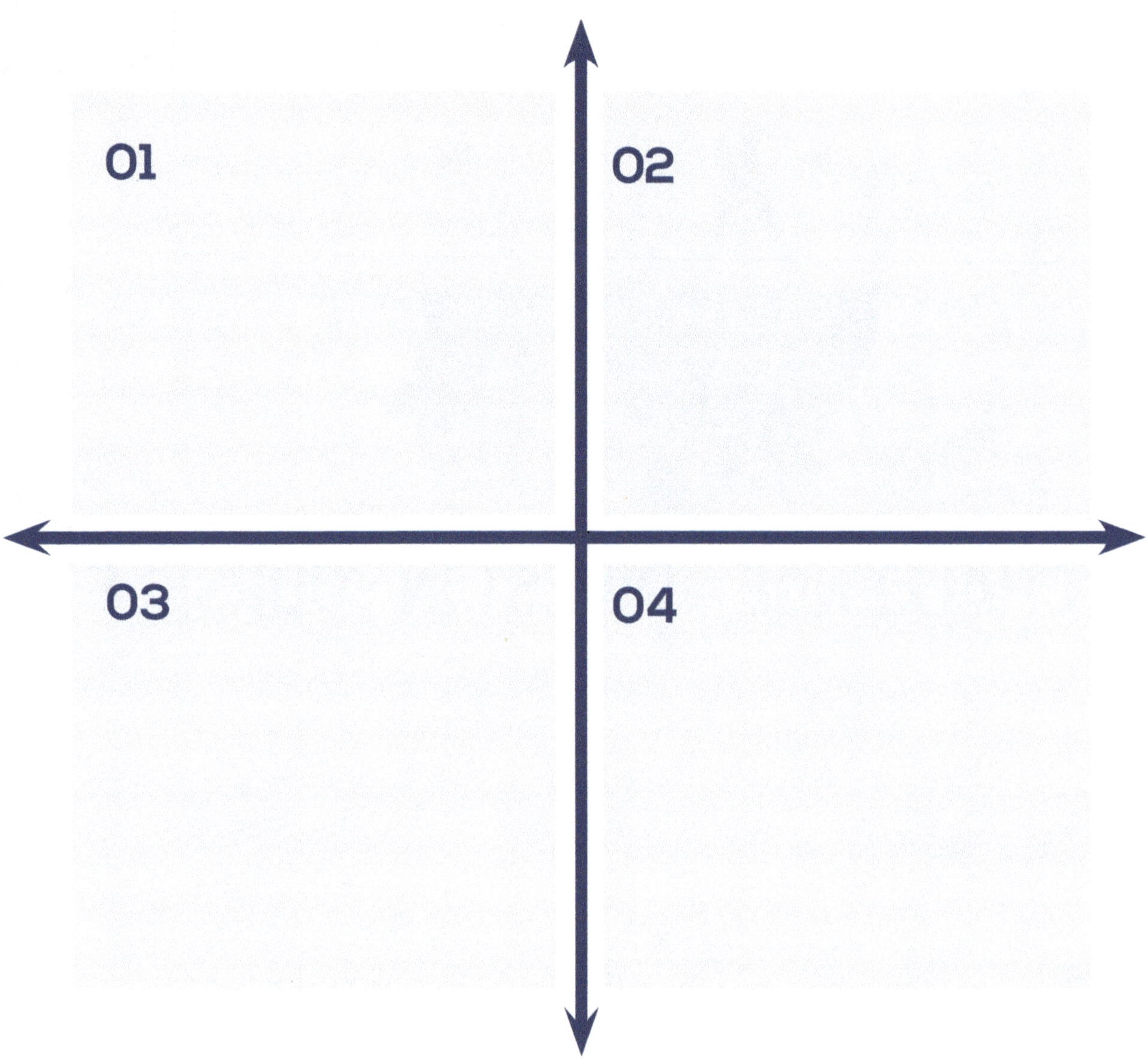

2. For the next 30 days, I want you to read at least one book related to the priority in the first box. If you prefer audio, you could listen to podcasts or YouTube content related to the focus in the first box for a minimum of 30 minutes each day. The goal is to help you organize your goals by priorities and provide you with the habit-building tool you need to help you reach your desired results.

3. After 30 days, re-evaluate. Don't practice every priority at once. After completing this challenge, you can move to the next priority box and repeat the process.

    ERVEN NELSON

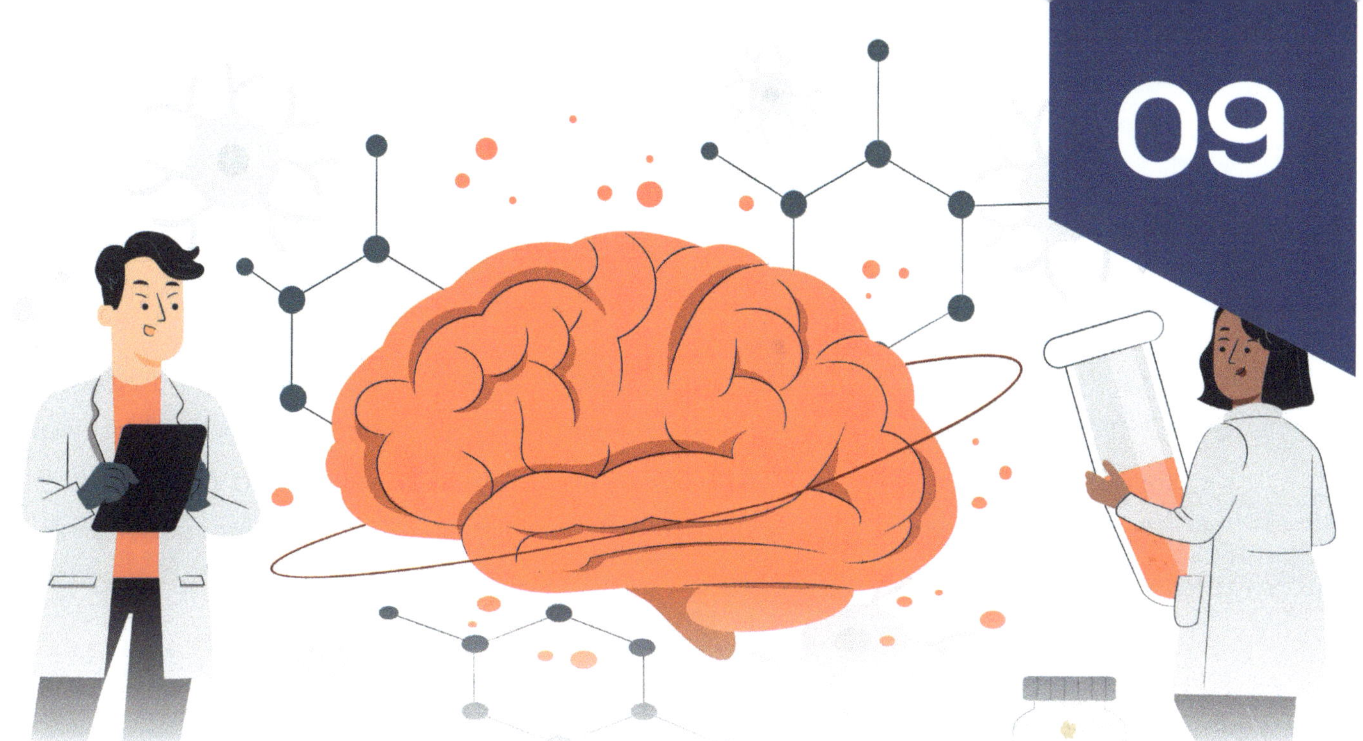

CHALLENGE – RECONDITION YOUR MIND

Comment:

Your environment, addictions, and past experiences do not define who you are. One of the oldest concepts of marketing, the rule of seven, says that a prospective buyer must hear an advertisement at least seven times before being "sold" on a product or service. Today, that number is much higher with social media and the internet. Subconsciously, you are advertising what you want to yourself. The goal is to recondition your mind to define your life how you want it to be.

Directions:

1. Choose the words to best describe the goal you want to accomplish. You must speak it into existence. Make sure the words you choose are definite. For example, you could say, "I am a doctor, a lawyer, a musician, a professional athlete, an educator, I will get the promotion at my job," or whatever other goal you desire.

____

____

____

____

____

2. Allot seven times throughout a typical day to recite your affirmation. For example, as soon as you wake up and before you go to bed at night. Other examples include when you use the restroom, at meals, when you brush your teeth, and commuting to and from work.

3. After 30 days, re-evaluate. An important note: reconditioning your mind to commit to a goal entirely is not an easy process, and saying the words aloud won't substitute hard work and focus.

CHALLENGE - EVALUATE YOUR NETWORK

1. In the columns below, take inventory of the people you interact with most. Examples of people you interact with are: friends, family, partners, suppliers, supporters, colleagues, vendors, spouses, mentors, and investors.

NAME	NAME

2. On the columns below, answer the following questions with (Y) for yes or (N) for no:

A. Do they add value to my life?

B. Do they support my ambitions, goals, or dreams?

NAME	A	B

If you answered no to anyone written in both columns above, consider reducing your footprint with them so you can be at your best for yourself, your loved ones, and your business.

ERVEN NELSON

3. After taking inventory of the people you interact with the most and identifying the ones you answered yes to the above questions, assess your relationship with them. This challenge requires both honesty and deep self-reflection.

On the lines below, answer the following questions about the people you answered yes to the previous questions:

I.   How can I help fulfill their needs with my skills, trades, time, or other resources?

II. Do I value our relationship?

III. Do I support their ambitions, goals, or dreams?

4. Now, you need to make it right. For example, if you find you're not valuing a relationship enough, ask yourself, "What can I do to reciprocate value to this person?" Write down your thoughts on the space below.

ERVEN NELSON

CHALLENGE - PREPARE FOR AN INTERVIEW

Comments:

Based on my five years of experience as a hiring manager, here are the top five things recruiters and employers look for in candidates.

Directions:

Conduct practice interviews in the same format as the real one. For example, if it's a face to face interview, ask a friend to meet and conduct a mock interview with you to practice answering questions in person. Choose a friend who is willing to give you honest feedback.

1. DO NOT Arive Late

- Arrive 10 minutes before the interview to anticipate traffic, weather, and loss in direction. It will also give you time to collect your thoughts and mentally prepare.
- Early arrival will show employers that you are responsible and possess good time-management skills.

2. Let Your Personality Shine

- Greet your interviewer with a friendly smile.
- Let your personality shine! In some cases, your credentials will not earn you a job opportunity if your personality does not fit their culture and team. Unfortunately, if you and another equally qualified candidate exceeded expectations during an interview, but there is only one position available for the role, the employer will pick the person they liked the most. The key is getting the interviewer to like you as a person just as they want your skills and experience.

3. Be Confident

- Think of an interview as just a conversation between you and the interviewer. Avoid stuttering and long pauses.
- Maintain eye contact and practice good body language.
- Try to be relaxed, but use a passionate communication style. One way to build your confidence is to conduct practice interviews in the same format as the real one. For example, if it's a face to face interview, ask a friend to meet and conduct a mock interview with you to practice answering questions in person. Choose a friend who is willing to give you honest feedback.

- ➤ Practice looking in the mirror and answering sample questions out loud.

4. Be Prepared

- ➤ Bring extra copies of your resume to the interview.
- ➤ Be ready to share highlights of your career journey for a minimum of five minutes.
- ➤ Prepare 2-3 questions to ask the interviewer.
- ➤ Make sure your clothes are ironed, clean, and presentable.

5. Use The SAPL Method

The SAPL method is a technique you can use to answer behavioral-based interview questions by discussing the situation, action, positive result of the situation you are describing, and the lesson learned during the process.

- ➤ **Situation:** Describe the situation first.
- ➤ **Actions:** Identify the steps you took to handle the situation.
- ➤ **Positive Result:** What were the results of your actions? Keep it positive. Avoid using a situation with a negative outcome. Talk about some numbers, percentages, or increases you can use when talking about your responsibilities and accomplishments.
- ➤ **Lesson Learned:** Give an example of a lesson you learned that didn't interfere with your ability to get the job done. Did the experience grow your skills?

SAPL Example:

Question: Tell me about a time you went above and beyond for a customer.

Situation:

One time, at my last retail job, an elderly customer who I had never seen before struggled to carry groceries in one hand while holding a cane in the other for balance and support while walking.

Actions:

First, I stopped the tasks I was performing at the time to acknowledge the customer immediately. Then, I asked for her name and offered to free up her hands from the shopping basket she was carrying instead of waiting for her to ask for help. She expressed that she was feeling muscle aches and fatigue but needed to buy a few grocery items for her grandkids visiting on the next calendar day. With her permission, I wrapped her arm around my shoulder to assist her in walking to her vehicle. I gave the customer a pen and paper to write a grocery list and offered to do the shopping for her. I wanted to ensure that someone else was fulfilling my role and adhering to the business needs, so I communicated with other team members over a headset that I would be spending additional time shopping for the customer. Finally, I loaded the groceries into her vehicle and thanked her for choosing to shop at my store instead of local competitors.

Positive Result:

The customer completed a survey explaining how she had an exceptional experience, contributing to positive store metrics. The customer is currently a regular customer who visits several times weekly, which is essential to sales and profit growth.

Lesson Learned:

The lesson from the scenario was that going the extra mile to make a customer's day leads to business success. Growing sales starts with the experience the customer receives in any business establishment. Since then, I've been striving to make someone's day a little brighter, inside and outside of work.

5 Sample Behavioral-Based Interview Questions:

1. Tell me about a time you went above and beyond for a customer.

2. Tell me about a time you failed. How did you deal with the situation?

3. Tell me about a time when you had to work closely with someone whose personality was very different from yours.

4. Describe a time when your team or company was undergoing some change. How did that impact you, and how did you adapt?

5. Give me an example of a time you managed numerous responsibilities. How did you handle it?

DISCUSSION QUESTIONS

1. What opportunities have presented themselves to you that you didn't take? Reflect on what held you back. What opportunities have you seized in the past that have been worth it?

2. What two words do you want people to associate with you?

3. Motivation is like drinking a double espresso: it gets you going for a while, but eventually you'll crash. When you feel motivated, suddenly you feel as if you can reach the results you desired instantaneously. How often has a motivational speech gotten you excited about going after your aspirations, only for you to be back to your old habits shortly after? The key is having the discipline to stay motivated and focused until you reach your desired results. What habits are you developing to stay motivated and focused on your desired results?

4. Goals give you direction, and the plan keeps you focused. Describe one short-term attainable goal you set to help you accomplish your long-term goal. Be specific. What progress are you making?

ERVEN NELSON

5. Strengths are things you can use to push yourself forward. Weaknesses are areas you need to improve on. What are your strengths and weaknesses? What steps are you taking to improve your weaknesses?

6. When someone asked if I wanted to meet at a pricey restaurant with tablecloths, I would respond with, "I don't have an appetite." Have you ever experienced a similar situation? If so, what are you doing to get back on track with your finances?

7. What's something you stressed about recently that you realized was perceived as life-threatening and not truly life-threatening?

8. What skill or trade do you possess with value and potential? How are you investing in yourself?

9. How are you contributing to society? How does it make you feel?

10. What is the difference between an asset and a liability?

11. After reading this book, did you discover something new about yourself that you weren't aware of beforehand? How does it make you feel?

About The Author

ERVEN NELSON

is an author, leadership coach, and speaker focused on self-help. Despite the struggles of growing up as one of six kids raised by a single mother, he managed to graduate high school and complete two years of technical college. Erven is the founder of the Seven Lessons Foundation, which helps future generations build character and wealth through mentoring and financial empowerment. His integrity, positivity, humility, and passion for excellence have earned him seven promotions in just 8 1/2 years at Wawa, a Fortune 500 corporate retail company. When Erven isn't listening to audiobooks or writing, he is probably composing music.

CONNECT ONLINE

WWW.IAMERVENNELSON.COM

Bring Erven to Your Organization

For all speaking inquires, contact bookervennelson@gmail.com. You and your organization can connect with Erven and his message by engaging him for:

- ➤ Keynote Events
- ➤ Youth Events
- ➤ Executive Team Meetings